# SHOTS

PHOTOGRAPHY BY **WILLIAM LINGWOOD**

# SHOTS
## BEN REED

RYLAND
PETERS
& SMALL

LONDON  NEW YORK

First published in the
United States in 2007
by Ryland Peters & Small, Inc.
519 Broadway
5th Floor
New York, NY 10012
www.rylandpeters.com

10 9 8 7 6 5 4 3 2 1

ISBN-10: 1 84597 502 2
ISBN-13: 978 1 84597 502 9

Printed in China

Senior Designer **Paul Tilby**
Commissioning Editor **Miriam Hyslop**
Senior Editor **Catherine Osborne**
Production Manager **Patricia Harrington**
Publishing Director **Alison Starling**

Stylist **Helen Trent**
Photographer **William Lingwood**

**NOTE**

Whilst enjoying putting this book into practice,
please bear your poor liver in mind. Even the most
hardworking of livers can only process one unit
(1 oz) of alcohol per hour. As a result and in
attempt to keep at least the odd wit about you,
limit your shot intake to one per hour!

# CONTENTS

6 down in one!
8 equipment and techniques
10 shaken
32 layered
50 built & straight up
64 index

# DOWN IN ONE!

The party drink with a kick—the shot—got its name from the receptacle from which it was, and still is, consumed—the shot glass.

Originally from Europe, the shot glass was most likely designed to contain lead shot. There is a claim that such glasses were first used to holster writing quills in the 1700s, but frankly the first story has a nicer relevance! In 18th-century England "firing" glasses were made with thicker glass bottoms so that they could withstand the banging on tavern tables that happened once toasts had been made, glasses raised and spirits consumed. The sound these glasses made when they were slammed down on the table resembled a musket being fired, hence their name.

In their early life shot glasses were used to dispense single spirits, either to sample the wares of early tavern owners or to propose a toast. However, as enterprising bartenders came up with more and more inventive ways to spice up the contents of the shot glass, the drink evolved into the many formats we see today—shooters, layered shots, and slammers.

Mixed over ice and strained into a shot glass, shooters are cool and refreshing. For a more discernible palate, layered shots not only look the part, they also hit the spot. The slammers of the group, spirits combined with carbonated ingredients, are slammed on the bar for dramatic effect and provide an excellent ice-breaker. Whatever you choose, it's sure to get your party started with a "bang."

# EQUIPMENT & TECHNIQUES

## Equipment

The first thing any aspiring bartender should acquire is a **measure (jigger)**. The useful modern dual-measure jigger measures both 2 oz. and 1 oz. (a double and a single measure).

The **shaker** is the second most important piece of equipment. The Boston shaker, half stainless steel, half glass, is great for a stylish performance, but a shaker with a strainer and twist-off cap also works well.

The **barspoon**, with its long spiralling handle, is useful for stirring drinks and the gentle pouring required for layered drinks. The "wrong," flat end can be used for muddling or crushing herbs, etc.

A **mixing glass** with strainer is used for making drinks that are stirred.

And last but not least, the small, sturdy **shot glass** is designed with one purpose in mind: getting what is usually a fairly high-alcohol drink from the glass into one's mouth with as little fuss as possible.

## Techniques

There are three basic types of shots—shooters, layered shots, and slammers. These are accomplished using several basic techniques: shaking, stirring over ice, layering, and building.

### Layering

To layer a cocktail, there are a couple of rules that need to be adhered to. First, and perhaps most obviously, choose liquors that will look dramatic when layered on top of one another in the glass. Secondly, layer each liquid in order of density—this means adding the heaviest spirits first, as they will sit at the bottom of the glass. The lower the proof in a drink and the greater the sugar level, the denser the liquid will be. Therefore, the sweetest and lowest proof liquid should be poured into the glass first. The higher the proof and the lower the sugar content, the lighter the spirit is. Be warned—this technique requires a steady hand. Pour your first ingredient into the shot glass. Pour your second down the spiral stem of a barspoon with the flat bottom resting on the surface of the liquid below.

## Shaking

Using a shaker is the most enjoyable way to make a shot, both for you and your guests. Add the ingredients to the shaker and fill it with ice. The shaking movement should be sharp and fairly assertive, but do remember to keep your hands on both parts of the shaker or at least a finger on the cap. Drinks containing egg white, cream, and juices should be shaken for slightly longer than the usual ten seconds.

## Building

The process of building a shot just requires adding the measured ingredients to the appropriate glass with perhaps a quick stir before serving.

## Make Your Own Simple Syrup

This is easy to make at home. Stir 2 cups of sugar into 1 cup of water and stir vigorously. Keep in a bottle in the fridge.

## Basic Rules

For each layered and built drink shots are calibrated at a total of 2 oz. Whereas for the shaken drinks, allow approximately 1/3 oz. less. This is owing to the extra dilution (or stretching) of the drink caused by shaking.

# SHAKEN

# APRICOT ROYALE

Adding a dash of champagne to each shooter not only lends a celebratory feel to the drink, the bubbles lift the flavors giving the drink a certain frivolity.

**1 scant oz. apricot brandy**

**⅓ oz. fresh lemon juice**

**1 dash simple syrup**

**⅓ oz. champagne**

Shake all but the champagne in a shaker filled with ice and strain into a shot glass. Top with champagne.

# BLUEBERRY AMARETTO SOUR

**1 oz. blueberry-infused Amaretto**

**⅔ oz. fresh lemon juice**

**1 dash Peychaud bitters**

Crush a handful of blueberries and leave them in a bottle of Amaretto until you can taste their influence, then decant the liqueur and strain them out.

Shake all the ingredients in a shaker filled with ice and strain into a chilled shot glass.

# VELVET HAMMER

**²/₃ oz. Cointreau**
**²/₃ oz. white crème de cacao**
**¹/₃ oz. heavy cream**

A light fluffy shooter with the orange of the Cointreau and chocolate from the cacao combining beautifully.

Shake all the ingredients in a shaker filled with ice and strain into a shot glass.

# VODKA ESPRESSO

**1 scant oz. vodka**
**Single espresso shot**
**¹/₃ oz. simple syrup**

Use freshly made espresso in this drink to put that extra spring in your step.

Shake the all ingredients in a shaker filled with ice and strain into a shot glass.

# ALABAMA SLAMMER

½ oz. sloe gin
½ oz. Southern Comfort
½ oz. Amaretto
⅓ oz. fresh orange juice

A cocktail immortalized in the film that every bartender loves to hate. What *Cocktail* did for bartending could only be countered by what *Titanic* did for ocean cruises.

Add all the ingredients to a shaker filled with ice. Shake sharply, strain into a shot glass, and serve.

# HORNY BEE (VX)

1 scant oz. Appleton Estate VX rum
⅓ oz. fresh lime juice
⅓ oz. runny honey

This drink can be sipped or shot, either way the honey will help this drink slip down your throat—you won't be pulling any faces after this shooter.

Stir the honey into the lime juice and run in a shaker. Once the honey is absorbed, add ice and shake sharply. Strain into a shot glass.

# KAMIKAZE

A great drink to get the party started. Easy to make, and even easier to drink, this is a low-maintenance shooter that does its job with minimum bother.

**1²⁄₃ oz. vodka**
**1 scant oz. fresh lime juice**
**1 scant oz. triple sec**

Add all the ingredients to a shaker filled with ice. Shake very hard, strain into two shot glasses, and serve.

# BAZOOKA JOE

For those with a sweet tooth, this shot will delight the palate.

Add all the ingredients to a shaker filled with ice. Shake and strain into a shot glass.

**½ oz. blue curaçao**
**½ oz. Baileys**
**½ oz. crème de banane**

# LEMON DROP

There are various ways to present this shooter. You can coat a lemon slice in sugar and lay it over the surface of the glass to bite into after the shot, or you can take it one step further and soak the lemon in Cointreau before coating it, then ignite!

**1 oz. lemon vodka**
**⅓ oz. Cointreau**
**⅓ oz. fresh lemon juice**
**a lemon slice, to garnish**

Add all the ingredients to a shaker filled with ice. Shake very hard and strain into a shot glass. Garnish with a lemon slice.

**⅔ oz. vodka**
**⅓ oz. lime cordial**
**⅓ oz. Cointreau**
**⅓ oz. raspberry purée**

Shake all the ingredients in a shaker filled with ice and strain into a shot glass.

# RASPBERRY KAMIKAZE

This drink doesn't have to be made with raspberries. It works with a number of flavors (and there are many!).

# PURPLE HAZE

1 white sugar cube
½ lime
2 oz. vodka
1⅔ oz. Grand Marnier
⅓ oz. Chambord each

The Purple Haze is a classic Kamikaze with a twist—a drink that belies its strength and will kick-start any evening's fun.

Put a sugar cube and the fresh lime half, cut into quarters, into a shaker and crush them together with a muddler or barspoon. Add the vodka and Grand Marnier. Fill the shaker with ice, then shake and strain the mixture into two chilled shot glasses. Drizzle the Chambord onto the drink and serve.

# DARK AND STORMY
# (WITH RASPBERRY)

1 scant oz. Appleton Estate VX rum
⅓ oz. fresh lime juice
⅓ oz. raspberry purée
chilled ginger beer, to top

A short variation on a long drink, you'll find this shot strangely addictive.

Shake the first three ingredients in a shaker, pour into a chilled shot glass and top with chilled ginger beer.

# NUTTY SURFER

½ oz. Frangelico
½ oz. cream
⅔ oz. Malibu

This shot will transport you to sunnier climes.

Shake all the ingredients in a shaker filled with ice and strain into a shot glass.

# SURFER ON ACID

Every now and again you come across a drink that doesn't sell itself well on paper—it just goes to show you should never judge a book by its cover.

Shake all the ingredients in a shaker filled with ice and strain into a shot glass.

½ oz. Jäegermeister
½ oz. Malibu
½ oz. pineapple juice

# DRAGON'S BREATH

Don't have more than one of
these as they can have quite
a kick. The absente top gives
it a refreshing edge.

²/₃ oz. lemon juice
½ oz. Chambord
½ oz. absente

Shake the lemon and the Chambord in a
shaker filled with ice and strain into a shot
glass. Layer the absente on top.

# ALL FALL DOWN

Tequila, rum, and coffee flavors
combine for a strong after-dinner shot.

½ oz. gold tequila
½ oz. dark rum
½ oz. Tia Maria

Add all the ingredients into a shaker filled with
ice, shake sharply, and strain into a shot glass.

# MELON BALL

An easy one to make, and even easier to consume.

Add all the ingredients to a shaker filled with ice, shake sharply, and strain into a chilled shot glass.

½ oz. **Midori**
½ oz. **vodka**
½ oz. **pineapple juice**

# BIKINI

A hint of orange and a tickle of strawberry, served nice and cold.

Shake all the ingredients in a shaker filled with ice and strain into a shot glass.

½ oz. **strawberry schnapps**
½ oz. **Grand Marnier**
½ oz. **vodka**

# THE ITALIAN JOB

This drink was created for Schweppes as a cocktail that explores how your mouth detects taste. Swill this around in your mouth and you should detect bitter, sour, and sweet tastes all rolled into one.

**1 scant oz. Amaretto**
**½ oz. fresh lemon juice**
**1 dash Campari**
**Tonic water (optional)**

Shake all the ingredients in a shaker and strain into a shot glass then add a dash of chilled tonic water, if liked.

# RUSSIAN QUALUDE

**½ oz. Russian vodka**
**½ oz. Frangelico**
**½ oz. Baileys**

This one was on the original Met Bar menu and was always popular.

Shake all the ingredients in a shaker filled with ice and strain into a shot glass.

LAYERED

# IRISH FLAG

²/₃ oz. green crème de menthe
²/₃ oz. Baileys
²/₃ oz. Grand Marnier

One of many great layered drinks that you see rolled out every St. Patrick's day.

Layer each ingredient on top of each other over a barspoon in a shot glass.

# ANGEL'S KISS

1¹/₃ oz. dark crème de cacao
2²/₃ oz. heavy cream

As the name suggests, this shot should soothe and caress.

Layer in order over a barspoon in a shot glass.

# BMW

Another one of those drinks that may not look that tempting on paper, but it certainly hits the spot!

²/₃ oz. **Baileys**
²/₃ oz. **Malibu**
²/₃ oz. **Jack Daniels**

Layer each ingredient on top of each other over a barspoon in a shot glass.

# FLAT LINER

1 scant oz. white Sambuca
8 dashes Tabasco sauce
1 scant oz. gold tequila

One for those of us that think that drinking shots should involve a certain amount of pain.

Layer each ingredient on top of each other over a barspoon.

# BJ # 2

²/₃ oz. white Sambuca
²/₃ oz. Baileys
²/₃ oz. whipped cream

Not the original recipe,
but still a hot favorite.

Layer each ingredient on top of the
other over a barspoon in a shot glass.

# ANGEL'S TIP

1¹/₃ oz. dark crème de cacao
1 oz. heavy cream

Just be careful the person who's
drinking the cocktail knows
there's a cherry lurking in the cream!

Layer in order over a barspoon and garnish
with a cherry.

# MEXICAN FLAG

²/₃ oz. Grenadine
²/₃ oz. green crème de menthe
²/₃ oz. Baileys

This shot's not too strong but like Mexican food it will leave a taste in your mouth for a while.

Layer each ingredient on top of the other over a barspoon in a shot glass.

# BABY GUINNESS

1¹/₃ oz. Kahlúa
²/₃ oz. Baileys

A tickler and easy to make, too.

Layer in order over a barspoon in a shot glass.

# BRAIN HEMORRHAGE

**1 oz. peach schnapps**
**1 scant oz. Baileys**
**1 dash grenadine, to dribble**

OK, so this is one of the silly ones. When made well, this is a truly disgusting looking shot but your adventurous spirit will be rewarded if you dare ...

Layer the Baileys on top of the peach schnapps in a shot glass. Dribble the grenadine through the Baileys so that it settles on the bottom of the glass and serve.

# CAR BOMB

**½ oz. Jameson whiskey**
**½ oz. Baileys**
**½ pint Guinness**

This one should really be reserved for those nights when you're drinking in a bar close to home.

Layer the first two ingredients in order into a shot glass, then drop it into the half pint of Guinness.

# SLIPPERY NIPPLE

Although this may sound like a bit of a comedy shot, the combination of Sambuca and Baileys slips down like liquid velvet.

Layer the Baileys gently on top of the Sambuca and serve.

**1⅓ scant oz. white Sambuca**
**⅔ oz. Baileys**

# AFTER SIX

**⅔ oz. Kahlúa**
**⅔ oz. crème de menthe**
**⅔ oz. Baileys**

A variation on the After Eight for those of you who are just too impatient to wait.

Layer in order or build into a shot glass.

# POUSSE CAFÉ

Pousse Café literally means "push coffee" and this was how it was originally served —as an accompaniment, to be sipped layer by layer alternately with the coffee.

**grenadine**

**dark crème de cacao**

**Maraschino liqueur**

**curaçao**

**green crème de menthe**

**Parfait Amor**

**Cognac**

In a tall shot glass or pousse café, layer a small measure of each of the ingredients, one on top of the other (see page 8).

# DETOX

The combination of peach schnapps, cranberry juice, and vodka is one that has been toyed with before, but layering the well-chilled ingredients in the Detox allows the luxury of tasting them one at a time.

**1 scant oz. peach schnapps**

**⅓ oz. cranberry juice**

**1 scant oz. vodka**

Layer each ingredient on top of the other over a barspoon in a shot glass.

# B52

The B52 has reached the lofty peak of being regarded a classic within the world of layered drinks. This shot is best drunk after dinner, as it has a tendency to take the palate by storm.

**1 scant oz. Kahlúa**
**½ oz. Baileys**
**½ oz. Grand Marnier**

Layer each ingredient on top of each other over a barspoon in a shot glass.

# POUSSE CAFÉ 2

Another real labor of love. The Pousse Café 2 requires a steady hand and a steely resolve—especially if your guest pays little shrift to your hard work and chooses to down the drink "in one!"

In the order given, layer a small measure of each of the ingredients, one on top of the other, in a liqueur or tall shot glass.

**grenadine**
**anisette**
**Parfait Amor**
**yellow Chartreuse**
**green Chartreuse**
**curaçao**
**Cognac**

# BUILT
## & STRAIGHT UP

# TEQUILA SLAMMER

The Tequila Slammer is the ultimate machismo drink and one that needs to be handled with care. This one is as likely to be imbibed for the sensation as the taste. A variation is to replace the gold tequila and champagne with silver tequila and lemonade.

**1²/₃ oz. gold tequila**
**1²/₃ oz. chilled champagne**

Pour both the tequila and the chilled champagne into an old-fashioned glass with a sturdy base. Hold a napkin over the glass to seal the liquid inside. Sharply slam the glass down on a stable surface and drink in one go as the drink is fizzing.

# STOLI SHOT

A shot of Stoli will not only revive you, it will also put a smile on your face. Ensure that both the vodka and the shot glass are arctic cold.

**2 oz. frozen Stolichnaya**

Pour the Stoli straight from the freezer into a chilled shot glass.

# RUSSIAN ROULETTE

The Russian Roulette is as much fun to make as it is to drink. Not to be recommended to anyone with a love for elaborate facial hair.

**1 scant oz. Galliano (plus extra for the lemon)**
**1 scant oz. chilled Stolichnaya**
**granulated sugar**
**a lemon wedge**

Layer the two ingredients in a shot glass. Coat a lemon wedge with sugar, douse with Galliano and light. Once the flame is out, drink the shot and bite in to the lemon.

# BRAVE BULL

Tequila and coffee work well together. Remember, the better the tequila the better the drink.

**1 oz. Kahlúa**
**1 oz. gold tequila**

Build or layer in order in a shot glass.

# LOS TRES AMIGOS

**a lime wedge**
**2 oz. gold tequila**
**a pinch of salt**

The salt, tequila, and lime method is as ubiquitous as the Margarita when it comes to tequila. Recite the immortal words: "lick, sip, suck"—and enjoy!

Hold the lime wedge between the thumb and index finger. Pour the tequila into a shot glass and place the glass in the fleshy part of your hand between the same thumb and finger. Place a pinch of salt on the top of your hand next to the shot glass. In this order: lick the salt, shoot the tequila, and suck on the lime.

# SUBMARINE

Forget those age-old constraints of spirit and chaser standing alone. Opt instead for the energy-saving Submarine and allow the tequila to seep gently from under its upturned shot glass and mingle with the beer before it hits the palate.

**2 oz. gold tequila**
**bottle of Mexican beer**
**(such as Sol)**

Pour the tequila into a shot glass. Place the shot glass in an upside down beer glass so that it touches its base. Turn the beer glass the right way up so that the shot glass is upside down but the tequila is still inside. Gently fill the beer glass with the beer and serve.

## AFTER EIGHT

1 scant oz. Kahlúa

1 scant oz. white
crème de menthe

Try keeping both ingredients in the fridge prior to serving these shots.

Build all the ingredients into a shot glass.

2 oz. Arette Blanco
Tequila (chilled)

1 cucumber slice,
soaked in lime juice
and sprinkled with
chili powder

## EL COYOTE

A great tequila that's popular in London, but sure to go global.

Drink the tequila and then eat the cucumber!

# SANGRITA

This drink is the perfect way to savor a fine tequila. Try varying the Sangrita mix by adding different amounts of orange juice and spices.

Pour the tequila into a shot glass. Add the remaining ingredients to a separate shot glass and stir gently. The tequila should be tasted first, followed by the Sangrita mix.

**2 oz. Añejo Tequila**

**Sangrita mix:**
**2/3 oz. fresh orange juice**
**2/3 oz. tomato juice**
**1 dash fresh lime juice**
**1 dash grenadine**
**2 dashes Tabasco sauce**
**1 dash Worcestershire sauce**

**1 oz. lime cordial**
**1 oz. Baileys**

# CEMENT MIXER

Not the best tasting shot in this book but whatever doesn't kill you, is only going to make you stronger.

Build both ingredients into a shot glass.

# DEPTH CHARGE

This beer-liquor combo usually comes in
larger sizes, but in the interest of responsible
drinking it's been lowered to a half a shot and
a half a pint.

### 1 scant oz. Drambuie
### ½ pint of lager (preferably light beer!)

Pour the Drambuie into a shot glass and gently
lower into the half pint.

# EDMUNDO

You may want to order a beer chaser with this
one to sluice with after. Coffee grains get stuck
between the teeth—so not a good look.

### 2 oz. chilled Bombay Sapphire
### a lemon wedge, coated with ground coffee and sugar

Pour the gin into a chilled shot glass, bite the
lemon and pour the gin into your mouth. Swill
all the ingredients and swallow.

# INDEX

## A

After Eight 58
After Six 44
Alabama Slammer 16
All Fall Down 26
Angel's Kiss 35
Angel's Tip 38
Apricot Royale 12

## B

B52 48
Baby Guinness 41
Bazooka Joe 19
Bikini 28
BJ # 2 38
Blueberry Amaretto
   Sour 12
BMW 36
Brain Hemorrhage 43
Brave Bull 54
Built and straight up
   50–63

## C

Car Bomb 43
Cement Mixer 61

## D

Dark and Stormy 22
Depth Charge 62
Detox 46
Dragon's Breath 26

## E

Edmundo 62
El Coyote 58

## F

Flat Liner 36

## H

Horny Bee 16

## I

Irish Flag 35
Italian Job, The 31

## K

Kamikaze 19

## L

Layered shots 32–49
Lemon Drop 20
Los Tres Amigos 57

## M

Melon Ball 28
Mexican Flag 41

## N

Nutty Surfer 25

## P

Pousse Café 46
Pousse Café 2 49
Purple haze 22

## R

Raspberry Kamikaze
   20
Russian Qualade 31
Russian Roulette 54

## S

Sangrita 61
Shaken shots 10–31
Slippery Nipple 44
Stoli Shot 53
Submarine 57
Surfer on Acid 25

## T

Tequila Slammer 53

## V

Velvet Hammer 15
Vodka Espresso 15

## CONVERSION CHART

Measures have been rounded up
or down slightly to make measuring
easier. The key is to keep ingredients
in ratio.

| IMPERIAL | METRIC |
| --- | --- |
| 1 dash | 5 ml |
| 1/3 oz. | 10 ml |
| 1/2 oz. | 15 ml |
| 2/3 oz. | 20 ml |
| 1 scant oz. | 25 ml |
| 1 oz. | 30 ml |
| 1 1/2 oz. | 40 ml |